She Holds The Sun

Ashley Coady

BookLeaf
Publishing

India | USA | UK

Presentation by *BookLeaf Publishing*

Web: www.bookleafpub.com

E-mail: info@bookleafpub.com

ISBN: 9789363319486

First edition 2024

To My Darling.

ACKNOWLEDGEMENT

There are so many people to thank. Greg, for your constant support & encouragement to be the best version of myself. Katie, for giving me literally a decade's worth of encouragement to pursue my poetry. My family, for always supporting me & my passion. Special thanks to Neil Hilborn & the Writer's Circle family for reminding me I am a poet after all.

PREFACE

We look for progress, not perfection.

Change of State

The thing they don't tell you about blooming
is there's never really a stopping point
There's no limit for how high you can grow
stalks & stems only go so far
But you, darling, are a flourish
you're daffodil daydreams mixed with medicine
Sunflowers that never actually know
which way they're supposed to grow
Darling,
you are magic beanstalk
you are castle that lives in the sky
the clouds are there to do your bidding
& even if you choose to use them to hide
I will find your smile in rays of light,
I will find you in sunshine
Because you, darling,
are the epitome of warmth
The textbook definition of what it means to love
& be loved
You are miraculous & endless
A watercolor daydream
I will find you
in the warmth

Fade By Accident

Put my heart & organs inside another body
one that isn't actively eating itself as
an impact of my decisions
It is easier to run from the consequences
than it is to sit with a plate
I know I have a guardian angel,
but I think the universe stopped cooking for me
Or maybe I stopped allowing myself to be fed
this feeble attempt at living
this downside of make believe that I'm alright
& I know the doctor is worried
from the lack of gas in this machine
Let's blame the too high vitamin d
it's easier than shifting it onto myself
when I'm at risk of fading out

No Goddess Here

If my skin had turned purple
you would have called it a sunset
Would have said you made me look pretty
because I wouldn't listen
An empty threat holds control
when you don't know if the threat will ever
become real
You can't trust your own memory
so you chose to mess with mine
A waterfall kaleidoscope
a shimmer fallen to splinters
You never called me pretty
unless you created the mirage

The Excuse of Trying Again Tomorrow

When the doctor looks at me,
I know this isn't okay
that I am allowing myself to decay
That no matter how nonchalant I am
this problem is making my bones want to eat
themselves
No wonder tattoos hurt so much
Not enough fat between skin &, well,
anything
When the doctor looks at me in that way,
there is no more room for jokes
No more room for I'll get better at this tomorrow
I am turning walking corpse
I am girl on fire dousing herself out
You can't drink a cup of coffee
& treat it like a meal
Sure, you can pretend
but eventually the facade has to be given up
The doctor looks at me
like I don't realize how serious this is
I wonder if my discomfort is palpable
if this embarrassment can be clenched between
fists
I am grasping for anything to hold onto

& all I can find are my bedsheets
because it is easier to stare at the ceiling
than it is to make myself feel
the echo inside my stomach
I have allowed this hollow to take
me from the inside out
If you put your head against my chest
I am worried all you will hear is this vast
nothingness
I am the captain sitting atop the mast,
willing the boat to fill to avoid this inevitable
shipwreck
The doctor makes it clear it's known I'm trying
& I wonder if they think I'm treating
this as a joke
when I know my bones are turning over
when I know the empty space behind my navel
deserves to be filled
If you put your head against my stomach
all you will hear is the void,
it's the only thing that echoes back

You Always Swore On Your God OR I Won't Swear On Your God

I thought this was a good idea
until you brightened the dark parts
Highlighted the conflicts without
offering a resolution
There is no reprieve here
No holy prayer, only control
A threat of conversations being recorded for
playback,
to show in the past I said something different
because opinions weren't allowed to change
Recordings a means to discount & invalidate
to prove wrong what he wanted to be right
There was a light in the dark but
it took me to the center rather than an exit
A spin of a circle of words
purposefully making me dizzy
so I'd spit onto myself
Prove myself to be unsound,
spun around to catch myself in my own lie
when all I did was alter a decision
choose to change an opinion
There is no reprieve here,

only documentation
His want of proof to show I'm a raging madman
for wanting to refuse
for misremembering or wanting something
different
There is no light here
only an attempt to create ravings
to put me back in the dark
An altered perception,
the need for an unbruised ego
This is what it's like for someone to play God
when they can never reach Him

Repent, Repeat

If I weigh myself today
the scale will still say I am nothing
When the doctor sees you weigh ninety-six
pounds
fully clothed, shoes on,
you will want to crawl inside of yourself
You will want to shower in the dark
will want to stay clothed in front of your
boyfriend
Why should anybody see you naked when
you can't stand the sight of yourself
You will spend days, maybe even weeks,
obsessing over the fact you haven't
weighed this little since you were thirteen
You are twenty-eight now
your body has been a scaled yo-yo for the past
twenty years
I have tried calling out but all I found strength
for
was crawling back inside of my body
I tell myself to keep the lights on in the shower,
that the flicker of a candle will make me
nauseous
I imagine undressing & then redressing out of
fear of how my boyfriend will look at me

it is easier to keep these visible bones to myself
I have been a yo-yo on a scale for twenty-years
If I can get to one-hundred pounds by Christmas,
maybe people will stop looking at me like
I'm dying

If Jesus Could Rise Again, Why Can't Grandma?

My seven-year-old mouth is a drunk text on
autocorrect
What nobody tells you is grief will always sneak
out
There's a difference between seeing a dead body
for the first time
& seeing the dead body of someone you love
My seven-year-old mouth is the original
autocorrect
Look, you won't be able to tell me what I want
to hear
Language is a fickle thing
I wonder how many ways there are to say
"I'm grieving" without others knowing
like
"I have your doughnut recipe on my desk
but I was never taught how to make it"
or
"I keep seeing his face"
or
"I still have that number in my phone"
or
I'm going to crawl into the mouth of
seven-year-old me

I'll come out not curious,
not poet, not me
I'm going to crawl into the mouth of
seven-year-old me
& pretend I was never in the waiting room
& pretend I never saw you
& pretend
& pretend
& pretend
& pretend I am magician
I am egg hunter
I am the then & now
I am the weight of everything gone & the
nothing
of what never was
My seven-year-old mouth is a drunk text on
autocorrect
If I crawl into my mouth,
will you come back out?

Maybe Then, Maybe Not Now

Maybe in another life I am easier to love
Not so headstrong or forthright,
not the things that make me, me
not the thoughts that cause fights
or withholding information & getting told
I act worse than a child
Would have stopped drinking coffee & tea
stopped having mints & cough drops & candy
Would have allowed forced restrictions
Would have listened instead of having his voice
ring in my head two years later,
a dull roar
Wouldn't have panic attacks over food he
made me feel guilty for eating
doughnuts, pizza, fries,
coffee, tea, sweet treats,
dinner with my family,
ice cream, tater tots, anything he claimed would
rot my teeth
Maybe in another life I'd be easier to love
if I brushed my teeth until the enamel came off
if I bleached my hair until it fell out
if I scrubbed away the acne until I didn't have
any skin

if I went for more walks
Maybe if I flossed, or shaved the
back of my head more
or maybe if I moderated until I weighed nothing,
I already weigh nothing
Maybe in another life I am easier to love
because I never met him

Trauma Is A Deletion

The void is on call collect
for the fifth time this week
Mailbox is full
you don't want to give the void any more space
than it has already taken
so you don't delete any messages
Tried sifting through them,
but the words made you sad
Your hand became a machine
a robotic arm attached to you
pressing the number over & over &
over & over & over
Until all the messages are
gone

The Poet Describes Herself
As A Butterfly

If you hold a butterfly
you have to learn not to crush it
A beautiful specimen, yes, but sometimes
beauty is delicate
Their wings could crumble like paper
& we wouldn't want that
This brightly colored, delightfully patterned
thing deserves more
than to be plucked from the sky
& clenched too tightly
A broken leg, a ruptured wing, a
bent-at-an-odd-angle antenna
If you hold a winged insect
your only intention should be to help it be able
to fly
A flutter, a dip,
anything that is the opposite of crushing

I Will No Longer Tell You I'm Sorry

I will no longer tell you I'm sorry
because, contrary to what you believe,
I never had to be
Never had to swallow down pretend okay
when I was scared
Never should have willed myself to stay frozen
when my entire body wanted to be free
No,
I will not tell you I'm sorry
I no longer want to classify myself as a liar
my teeth are broken enough
& I don't need the threat of your fist splitting my
lip
So, no,
I will no longer accept your apologies
Will no longer pretend I believe it
when you say you're just joking
No,
this is my story
& there is no more room for lies here
No more room for you or for us
in this sacred narrative
Your faceful of apology will have to stop
blooming,

your mouth is full of dead sprouts
& I truly believe you should keep the threat of
your hands
to yourself
This is not a joke
This is not an insurance policy to keep you away
No,
this is me saying I will not lie
I will not stay
I will no longer apologize for control
that you only pretend to be

Cracked Like An Egg Yolk

& darling, when I say this starvation is
unintentional
we both know it isn't
My mind is an obelisk
believes it's keeping me safe from the inside out
& darling, I know,
I know you can see the dip of a soup kitchen in
my clavicle
because I know how to feed everybody except
myself
& I know, I know
my ribcage is a set of piano keys
but at least this means I can still make music
If I become an absence of sound
how will I remain
& I know this starvation is unnecessary,
unhealthy even
This lump of wet meat that's supposed to be my
brain
believes I should continue on empty
because if I am empty there is nothing
inside of me
& if there's nothing inside of me this
obelisk can know for a fact it will not be sick
& darling, I will never ask you

to play music on my bones
but, I was wondering if you'd be willing to
share your fries with me?

The Art Of Being A Garden

I am watercolor sunset
a river of sunflowers along a shore bank of
daffodils
A calamity people believe needs
to be fixed
An ostracized breath of nothing
a doomsday machine that keeps going
Teach me to snorkel & I'll find a new home
I've already taught myself the art
of treading water
The art of staying alive because
I want to be alive
The art of watercolor painting
using old paints & dirty water,
The art of reusing the old
& making something new

Within My Chest

& yet it moves
The Earth beneath our feet even
though we can't feel it
I keep being told that my legs
are too weak for me to stand
& I am tired of always having to
prove so many people wrong
Like my glow stick heart is an
attraction for someone to snap
a utopia the unholy crave & desire,
the pentacle they live for
I am crucible, the crumbling of euphoria
The crumbling so many of the unholy desire
& burn for
I am glow stick heart, the one
too many people have tried to
snap

The Tale of Purple Hair Dye
& Food Poisoning

The holidays without a narcissist are strange
There isn't anything you can do wrong now
because there is nobody to tell you
what you are doing is wrong
You don't have to welcome them into your
home,
don't have to redye your hair
Nobody to say you don't love them
because you had food poisoning on New Years,
that how dare you throw up the food they bought
& waste the money
Nobody to say you don't love them
because you shut your door instead of leaving it
open
Having a holiday after spending many with
a narcissist requires unlearning
You can wear your hair up instead of down,
if you want to
You don't have to paint your nails
or wear hoop earrings
or dress a certain way,
if you don't want to
No unnecessary conversations about
adult braces or acne cleansers

Your image is not to paint somebody else a saint,
you are not a projected picture
Art is messy & if you're going to be a
masterpiece
then you need to act like one
You don't have to look pretty
but you do have to make yourself feel something
Even if all you feel is off

Learning How To Be A
Home

The only thing I eat for breakfast
are all the words going through my head
the doubts & the wants
the needs & the hopes
Darling this is how it looks when I try to
stop erasing myself
My body is a caving in house
but I'm learning how to not
let it be haunted
Learning what it means to
provide nourishment & love
I know I cry a lot
but darling this is just my emotions
coming out through my eyes
because where are they supposed to go
This tired frame is fatigued enough
without finding more space for me
Without moving spoon to mouth
when words alone won't keep me fed

Cover Me Up

Cover me in stickers
If I'm going to relive my trauma
I might as well make it more fun
or at least mask it as something
more fun to be around
Make my inner child happy
& adult me giggle
& inner teenage me roll my eyes
because these are the things I spend my money
on
The things that make me happy
The things that make me glad
to still be alive

Caught Outside

I am dismal, ceiling stars in a bag
I am holy universe who forgot her coat
I do not want to get lost in you
The part they don't tell you about healing,
is what you like in sex changes
You will become softer
You will become less want & more desire
I no longer speak with my body
This is a lesson in reverency
The world is a bucking horse
& I am cherry red rage
I am the original forget-me-not
Navel a birdbath, clavicle a swimming pool
I am sunshine rage & pale daffodils
I am sunflowers scorched before blooming
Self-sabotage is no longer my middle name,
I am not fluent in that language anymore
I am unraveling the strings of destiny
I am lightning & will make shadows surrender
Holy universe my darling, where is your coat?
Some bridges are better off being burned
& I am bored with being sad
I am burnt matches & discarded tanks of
gasoline
I, am dismal, the original forget-me-not

a repressed transgression, a relentless starlit
beauty
Oh holy universe, my love, where is your coat?
There is safety in resurrection
but you will not find that here
A ghost inside of a city that only sleeps
a primal taste of this sunshine desire
I am dismal, full of stars
Holy universe how can I be allergic to dust
when I am made of it?
The thing about healing is you're never told
the static doesn't stop, the bees keep coming
Let me show you what it's like
to breathe underwater
Oh holy universe I lost my coat
This is a lesson in reverency
Oh holy universe, how do I get her back?
The one on the other side of this healing
the one not clouded in purple rage
the one who never stopped humming
I have a list of things I've forgotten
& she's on top of every one
O holy universe, sing me to sleep
the birds will not recognize me as a home
I, am just beginning to see myself as a home
I am a torn raincoat, sunflowers swinging
A velvet sunset is where you can find me
when I'm not hiding inside my own clavicle
Darling, holy universe,

dismal stars in a bag
This is what it means to wake up
This is what it means to try again
This is what it means,
to find your coat

A Door Left Swinging

I fit my thumb in the space under my collarbone
& wonder when will it be enough
how many excavated bones will it take
to treat myself with kindness
How many dismissed hunger signals
until I am no longer a soup kitchen
but rather feeding myself
I am a success in motion
but if I faint the motion will be downward
The motion is already I don't know how
I'm going to bounce back this time
I am the nightwatch putting out the fire
then staying awake during the day
no wonder, I am so tired
No wonder self-care is an unfulfilled promise
I keep making myself every morning
Promise my body I'll feed it
Promise my brain I'll be nice to it
Promise my health it will get better
But how will I get better if the only
places I can be found are between
where bones creak
it is the only way I know how to speak anymore
I have been turning opposite of supernova,
but watch me continue to burn

Watch me take newborn steps & turn
this hollowed out ship around
There is no loving me in spite of myself,
but because I am myself
& every star I find I will carve into
the shape of my image
& eat it

A Loud Hourglass

There is no way to pause this
A slip of time or a use of it
Hours spent on adventures
or asleep in bed
Minutes spent on panic attacks
Seconds taken up by anxiety
all stacking up to result in hours
This quiet life lived loudly

I've Had Too Much Caffeine Today, I Don't Have A Title

& darling, if you're going to love yourself
I encourage you to ask questions & implore
consequences first
Darling, are you doing this for yourself
or other people?
You've been conditioned to stay for others,
but have you considered the option that
you're allowed to stay for yourself?
& darling, I know when people say
"I promise" you immediately think
"Don't make a lie you can't keep"
but what is the point of believing everything
is a lie when words aren't actually concrete?
Darling, you are miles from home
miles from any pair of arms that could hold you
but I encourage you to explore the idea
of holding yourself
You've spent thousands of dollars to come this
far,
so why stop here?
Why not make it to there?
To the out-of-budget house with the back
deck that has no stairs?
Why not pack up the U-Haul & leave?

If people choose to keep shoving you into a
cage it is because they did not expect you
to one day fight back
Darling when your feet hit the ground both
God & the Devil say "fuck"
Now darling this is not me saying you
did anything wrong but rather
you've done everything right
The fading bouquets, the unused concert tickets,
the empty passenger seat
Darling if they want to shove you into a cage
we will fight back
I've got matches & you've got gasoline
we'll burn the bridge even though we
don't know how to swim
You've got matches & I'll find gasoline
the city does not stand a chance,
will you burn it with me?
We'll siphon the gas from stalled out cars
& pick up extra matches from passing motels
Darling, I implore you to examine the risk of
the consequences of losing everything,
but you also stand the chance to gain anything
Encourage yourself darling,
to ask if this is truly for you
There is no going back into the cage
the way is paved with sunflowers instead of
a yellow brick road
Darling, when you decide this is truly,

& I mean truly a decision & leap of faith made
for you by you,
the lack of swim lessons won't matter
& darling, when you promise you love yourself
it is no longer a lie,
but rather a truth you can keep

Printed in the USA
CPSIA information can be obtained
at www.ICGtesting.com
LVHW021451030924
790000LV00029B/307